What's on My Plate?

Develop Understanding of Fractions and Numbers

Leah Morado

INFOMAX MATH READERS

Rosen Classroom™

New York

Published in 2015 by The Rosen Publishing Group, Inc.
29 East 21st Street, New York, NY 10010

Book Design: Mickey Harmon

Photo Credits: Cover Irina Mos/Shutterstock.com; pp. 3–24 (background) Evlakhov Valeriy/Shutterstock.com; p. 5 fuse/Getty Images; p. 7 Foodio/Shutterstock.com; p. 9 Bogdan Wankowicz/Shutterstock.com; p. 11 Factor41/Shutterstock.com; p. 13 sanse293/Shutterstock.com; p. 15 Gayvoronskaya_Yana/Shutterstock.com; p. 16 monticello/Shutterstock.com; p. 17 Elenadesign/Shutterstock.com; p. 19 francesco de marco/Shutterstock.com; p. 21 MSPhotographic/Shutterstock.com; p. 22 Christopher Boswell/Shutterstock.com.

ISBN: 978-1-4777-4609-7
6-pack ISBN: 978-1-4777-4611-0

Manufactured in the United States of America

CPSIA Compliance Information: Batch #WS15RC: For further information contact Rosen Publishing, New York, New York at 1-800-237-9932.

Contents

Let's Get Cooking!

I love to help my parents cook. It's important to make meals and snacks using healthy foods. I help my parents choose foods from different groups, such as fruits, vegetables, and grains.

By using a **variety** of healthy foods when we cook, we make sure we're eating a balanced **diet**. This means we eat the right amounts of healthy foods. My mom says having a balanced diet will help me grow healthy and strong. Getting enough exercise will help me stay healthy, too.

I often use fractions when I help my parents prepare healthy meals and snacks. Comparing fractions is one way to see if I'm eating the right amount of food from each group. A fraction has 2 parts: a numerator and a denominator.

$\frac{1}{2}$ ◀ numerator: number of parts taken or looked at

◀ denominator: total number of equal parts the whole is divided into

Comparing Plates

Fruits and vegetables are important parts of a healthy, balanced diet. Eating a salad with many different vegetables in it is a great way to eat a variety of healthy foods as part of a meal. I help my mom rip pieces of lettuce for a big salad. She's putting tomatoes, onions, carrots, and cabbage in the salad, too.

I want to compare the size of my salad with my dad's and my mom's. We each have salad on $\frac{1}{3}$ of our plates, but can we compare these fractions?

I can't compare these fractions because they're not parts of equal wholes. The plates, which are the wholes, are different shapes and sizes. That means each $\frac{1}{3}$ is a different size, too.

1/3
1/3
1/3

There's a good rule to follow to make sure you're eating enough fruits and vegetables. At every meal, make sure at least $\frac{1}{2}$ of your plate is made up of foods that come from these groups.

I use the same plates for breakfast and dinner. For breakfast, $\frac{1}{4}$ of my plate is filled with fruits and vegetables. For dinner, $\frac{1}{2}$ of my plate is filled with fruits and vegetables. Do I have more fruits and vegetables for breakfast or dinner?

By looking at the 2 plates, I can see that I eat more fruits and vegetables for dinner because $\frac{1}{2}$ is greater than $\frac{1}{4}$. I can write this using the **symbol** for "greater than," which is >.

$$\frac{1}{2} > \frac{1}{4}$$

Healthy Snacks

My mom often makes me a snack after school. Sometimes she cuts up pieces of raw vegetables for me to eat because they're very healthy. My favorite vegetables are peppers.

My mom cuts up some red peppers and some green peppers. She puts them on a rectangular plate. The green peppers take up $\frac{3}{5}$ of the whole plate, and the red peppers take up $\frac{1}{5}$. I know $\frac{1}{5}$ is less than $\frac{3}{5}$. I write that using the "less than" symbol, which is $<$.

I know $\frac{3}{5}$ and $\frac{1}{5}$ have the same denominator. You can compare fractions with the same denominator by looking at the numerators. The fraction with the smaller numerator is the smaller fraction.

$\frac{1}{5} < \frac{3}{5}$

Sometimes my mom prepares fruit for my after-school snack. My favorite fruit is an orange. It's fun to break an orange into parts, or sections. It's a way to practice using fractions! Oranges are also very healthy snacks. They can help keep you from getting sick.

My mom and I have oranges that are the same size. I eat $\frac{5}{7}$ of my orange, and she eats $\frac{5}{6}$ of her orange. I know I ate less than my mom because $\frac{5}{7}$ is less than $\frac{5}{6}$.

I can see that $\frac{5}{7}$ and $\frac{5}{6}$ have different denominators but the same numerator. When equal wholes are **divided** into more parts, it means each part is smaller. That's why $\frac{5}{7}$ is less than $\frac{5}{6}$ of the same whole.

$$\frac{5}{7} < \frac{5}{6}$$

Cooking with Grains

Foods made from grains are another important part of a balanced diet. These include bread, pasta, and rice. The healthiest foods in this group are made from whole grains. Whole-grain products are made using the entire **kernel** of a grain.

I know that $\frac{1}{2}$ of all the grains I eat should be whole grains. If the whole grains in my diet make up $\frac{1}{3}$ of all the grains I eat, is that enough? I know it's not enough because $\frac{1}{3}$ is less than $\frac{1}{2}$.

I can use these 2 equal rectangles to represent, or stand for, the whole amount of grains I eat in a day. This makes it easy for me to compare the fractions by looking at pictures of them.

$$\frac{1}{3} < \frac{1}{2}$$

When I help my parents cook, we often combine healthy foods from different groups. Pasta with tomato **sauce** is a dish that combines grains with vegetables. We put tomatoes, onions, and peppers in the sauce to include different kinds of vegetables.

My dad and I put our pasta on plates that are the same size. The pasta takes up $\frac{3}{4}$ of his plate. It takes up $\frac{3}{8}$ of my plate. I can look at the denominators of the fractions to see which is larger.

A circle divided into 4 pieces has larger pieces than a circle of the same size that's divided into 8 pieces. This is why $\frac{3}{4}$ is greater than $\frac{3}{8}$.

>
3/4 > 3/8

At the Store

Dairy products are some of my favorite foods. The dairy group includes milk and foods made from milk, such as yogurt, cheese, and ice cream.

Sometimes I go to the store to help my parents shop for healthy foods. I see wheels of cheese at the store that are the same size. There's $\frac{2}{3}$ of one wheel left and $\frac{2}{5}$ of the other wheel left. Which wheel has more cheese left? Is $\frac{2}{3}$ greater than or less than $\frac{2}{5}$?

You can look at the pictures of these fractions as well as their denominators in order to compare them. Do the wheels of cheese have to be the same size to compare the fractions?

?
$\frac{2}{3}$? $\frac{2}{5}$

Making My Lunch

I like to help my dad make my lunch. He often makes me a peanut butter sandwich on whole-grain bread. Peanut butter is a food that's rich in **protein**, which helps build and repair **tissues** in the body. Other foods that are rich in protein include chicken, beef, and fish.

My friend Riley and I both eat the same-size peanut butter sandwiches at lunch. She eats $\frac{1}{4}$ of hers, and I eat $\frac{3}{4}$ of mine. Did Riley eat more or less than I ate?

What methods can you use to compare these fractions?

$\frac{1}{4}$? $\frac{3}{4}$

A Healthy Family

Helping my parents cook is a fun way to learn about eating the right foods. It's also a fun way to learn about fractions. Math is a very important part of cooking!

I also stay fit by exercising. I play on my school's volleyball team, and I play soccer for my town. My parents like to exercise, too. We walk to the farm stand to buy healthy foods. Exercising and eating a balanced diet help us stay healthy.

A farm stand is a great place to buy a variety of fresh fruits and vegetables.

Glossary

diet (DY-uht) The food and drink that a person takes in.

divide (duh-VYD) To break into parts or shares.

kernel (KUHR-nuhl) A whole grain or seed of a cereal, such as wheat or corn.

protein (PROH-teen) A substance supplied by food that helps build and repair tissues in the body.

sauce (SAWS) A liquid served with food, often poured on top of the main dish.

symbol (SIHM-buhl) Something that stands for something else.

tissue (TIH-shoo) A group of cells of the same kind that come together to form the basic parts that make up a plant or animal.

variety (vuh-RY-uh-tee) A number or collection of different things.

Index